Look**Beyond**

Look**Beyond**

BY **DAVID MEYERHOF**

To order additional copies of this book, contact:
Xlibris Corporation
1-888-795-4274
www.Xlibris.com
Orders@Xlibris.com
118868

Contents

To my wife Carol, my son Matthew, my mother Miriam,
my father Walter, my brother Michael,
and all my former students

Acknowledgments

I would like to thank my wife Carol for her support and patience, my mother Miriam for her support, my son Matthew for his comments and ideas which were so helpful, JSTS Transcription Service, especially Victoria, for typing the original manuscript, Esther Wojicki for her ideas, Maria del Toro for her insight, and my other family members, friends and former students for their enthusiasm and interest.

When Your World is Turned Upside Down, How Do You Make It Right Side Up?

When your world is turned upside down,
What do you do—get out of town?
No, you take steps forward,
Keeping head up and toward.

Gather your forces all,
Stand up, stand tall.
Your heart must move along,
Prepare to right the wrong.

No one said it was easy or fair,
But you can fight it, if you dare.
Be ready to meet every turn.
From each action, you will learn.

So go forward still,
Push ahead, strengthen your will.
The world does await.
Now go, decide your own fate.

STEP UP TO THE PLATE

No one knows when or where
You will be called upon
To step up to the plate.
It may be soon, it may be late.

But you won't have a choice.
It will be you—your own voice.
Decisions will have to be made
Way out in the sun or close by in the shade.

The groundwork must be laid out.
Give it your all without a doubt.
You know, they are counting on you,
All that you say, all that you do.

So do not sit back and wait.
It's not your choice, it's your fate.
It's your world you must create.
So don't hesitate, step up to the plate.

No One Can Take It Away From You

No one can take away
What's inside you—it will stay.
That undeniable passion—that feeling,
Part of your soul—your being.

Are you quenching that thirst
Before you think it will burst?
Yours to keep, yours to hold,
Decidedly deep, decidedly bold.

Your love, your care
Goes beyond, fills the air.
Surrounded by your heart
From which you will never part.

Yours and yours alone,
That care that's really your own.
The sky may fall, the birds may cry,
But no one can take it away from you
By and by.

An Artificial Peace

The smiles shower upon her.
They flow and ebb, appear to endure.
The hands are out to help and hold,
The intent there so bold.

The flowers are cheery and bright.
The décor is really so right.
The food is superior and over the top.
The staff does not stop.

But as all is there
For the people—for the care,
It is the inside they cannot reach,
That which does beckon and beseech.

The horizon shows that house, that home,
Which is hers, her very own.
The only place to be
At peace and eternally free.

PAIN

When all that pain
Is greater than the gain,
What do you do?
Just sit there and turn blue?
No, my friend, that shall not be.
There's more to it, don't you see?
It comes with your mind,
Pushing forward, not getting behind.
The nagging, the pinching, the aching—
Why is it unrelenting, just taking?
Now you must fight tooth and nail,
Step up to the plate without fail.
It stabs like a knife
In each cell of your life.
Why does it take and take and take
When it's your life you must make and make and make?
The difficulty is there to see.
Just bear with it and let it be?
No, draw the line in the sand.
The power of love is at hand.

When She Cries Out

When she cries out in pain,
Is it a loss, or is it a gain?
Is progress being made
To move ahead, not fade?

It tears me up inside,
Eats at my dignity, my pride.
Can it please end now, now, now?
The question is how, how, how?

Steps must be taken to move ahead,
To extend, to get out of bed.
Is there more which can be done?
Can we find our place with the rising sun?

Is it all taking and not receiving?
Is this real or deceiving?
The challenge is plain to see,
So now uplift, be strong, and be free.

My Father's Hand

My father's hand did reach out
To hold her without a doubt.
Although he passed six years ago now,
He's still here to show us how.

So just as plain as day,
Across time, pointing the way.
There was no mistake or doubt,
The path was clear—the way out.

He always was the guide,
Giving us knowledge, showing us pride.
He is so deep in our heart,
To the end and from the start.

The light is there for us to see,
Take those steps, set us free.
Give us the power to get through,
Make her whole again so true.

TEARS TO FLOWERS

Can my tears nourish the flowers?
Will the hurt continue for hours?
Why does it go on and on and on nonstop—
Only pausing to breathe so I won't drop?

Somehow, sometime, and somewhere,
I must get through and clear the air.
My actions need to bring a change,
Bring back the familiar, not the strange.

Her life has been broken apart.
We must put it back again, like from the start.
Take one step, strengthen, then step once more.
Keep moving forward, open that door.

The answer lies within and without.
Bring back that smile, erase the doubt.
My tears will make the flowers grow,
Feel the sun's breath, and make her life flow.

HOPE ON THE HORIZON

Is it my imagination,
Or is it something real?
Is it something I can grasp,
Or something I can feel?

Time to make it the actual, the fact,
Upon which I can act.
The beginning of what was,
The reminder of what she always does.

The shoots of change are in the air
Due to all the love and care.
Appearances can be deceiving,
But now wonderful changes we are believing.

May she grow stronger each day,
May nothing get in her way.
She will make it happen, I know,
And that glowing smile will always show.

Incongruity

Why is it that some things are the same,
And others different—who's to blame?
But that's the way it goes,
Like a path—just what it shows.

When the "what is" becomes "how's that?"
Step aside, put the rabbit back in the hat.
Perhaps there's an order in our space,
The way things are, each in their place.

But we are all really human beings
With thoughts, feelings, ideas, and dreams.
So differences exist and abound.
Sometimes we are lost, sometimes we are found.

So let us work together now
And not worry about the when, where, and how.
We may not see eye to eye,
But in the end, we are really one, by and by.

Convoluted Soul

Are you that convoluted soul,
Inconsequential, without a goal?
Do you just sit and watch the traffic go by?
Do you just wish to write something in the sky?

Well, let me tell you, my friend,
There is a beginning, there is an end.
What you do in between is what matters,
So don't go around attracting mad hatters.

Don't be so twisted and wrapped up inside.
Get down to business, get with the guide.
You need to express what is pent up,
Figure out how far it went up.

We all go through that gut check.
We all have been on that shipwreck.
So grasp with all your might
That vision of life, that opening of light.

THE TEAM OF ARROGANCE AND IGNORANCE

Like birds of a feather,
Arrogance and ignorance go together.
They mirror each other in many a way,
Complement, intertwine all the day.

When you come upon this kind of boast,
You find little depth coast to coast.
Knowledge is only on the surface, not really there,
Rather prejudice shows up without a care.

The chest is all puffed up.
The brain is all stuffed up.
Where's the conscience, the thought, the feeling?
Did being self-centered just go through the ceiling?

So what have you achieved, acting so big?
We can see right through that appearance—like a wig.
Get off your high horse, come on down,
Get with humanity, join the people's town.

Welcome to the State of Denial

Welcome, one and all, to this unique place,
Where truth is not believed, not in this space.
Where reality is not allowed,
Where actuality is disavowed.

We all have been there.
We learned it's not our daily fare.
We've been there for a while,
Enough to throw it in the round file.

There are some who live in this state.
They go through and just close the gate.
Such a sad state of affairs,
Where the truth produces only blank stares.

I advise, do not travel there.
You'll regret it, if you dare.
We must be grounded in the plausible, the real
And avoid the false bravado with heartfelt zeal.

STRUGGLE

Is this what it's all about?
A world of uncertainty and doubt?
Is it something we cannot know,
Or something from which we cannot grow?

Wrong, my friend, and wrong once more.
Free your mind, even the score.
Time to go deep, reach inside,
Find the way, true and tried.

Now make that clenched fist.
Awake your power through the mist.
Use your strength, your pride,
Mark your steps, embrace the guide.

Over the barriers we go,
Into the truth we must know.
The fight has just begun.
We see far, we see our sun.

FORWARD OR BACKWARD

So what's it going to be—
Two steps forward or nothing to agree?
Time to make that choice,
Plunge into emptiness or exalt your voice.

Make that imperious move.
Show all that you can prove.
Your worth is beyond compare.
Your dignity shines as you dare.

Get with what's in motion,
The direction more than a notion.
Feel that stepping up of the pace,
The crescendo of rising up we all face.

So take what's higher than you,
Bring it close, make it true.
You know we're not letting go
Until the world is ours—see that red glow.

STEEL YOURSELF

It's time to steel yourself.
Stop being drawn into the realm.
Don't be taken for granted.
Realize the seeds are not yet planted.

Grow up, act mature.
Look up, ignore the lure.
It's time to move on.
Don't turn back, it's gone.

Get a hold of your real self.
Put those feelings back on the shelf.
Become a better you.
I think you know what to do.

Passion will come into play,
No matter what you do, no matter what you say.
So it's time to take those steps ahead.
No need to follow, no need to be led.

THE FUTURE

What about the future?
What does it portend—
A new beginning or an inglorious end?
A place of rebirth and flowery grace,
Or a shadowy inferno, a damning place?

Are we not imbued with destiny unveiled?
Are we not letting our spirits be derailed?
We cannot flounder or fall on the ground.
There's so much to learn, so much to be found.

Our hearts must go ahead.
Our desire for knowledge must be fed.
There is no time to stop or delay.
We are bursting with pride, we will not stray.

We grasp with all our might
That uplifting passion, that brilliant light.
We climb the tallest tower, the highest peak,
Our steps of life, our future is what we seek.

SILENCE

We listen to the shadows of silence,
Yet I hear the babbling of the spring.
Perhaps the fresh permeates the frost,
So I may know that I am not lost.

THE DAY IS SLIPPING AWAY

Where this day went, I do not know,
Into what and how did it go?
Will it be rough or smooth?
Will it fit into the groove?

Perhaps brightness will appear,
Or there will be darkness and fear.
Away we go down that beaten road,
Away we travel with an unforgiving load.

I want to hold onto the feelings, the thoughts,
And get rid of the pressure, the oughts.
So what's the matter with such a way?
Why won't it last, why can't it stay?

My hands are plaintive and kind.
Is this the answer I can find?
The here and now beckon my touch
And absorb my senses so much.

Here, But Not Here

I've been here before.
I know the street, the house, the door.
But am I really here?
I just don't know, I fear.

The familiarity is really striking.
Alas, my senses have gone hiking.
I want the feeling, the touch,
But it's not there, not that much.

I'm caught betwixt and between.
The sky shows gray, the clouds speak mean.
Thoughts travel by,
Intentions ask why.

I fly, I land, I fly,
I act bold, not shy.
No anchors are holding me,
So why are my wishes numb, not free?

SPIRIT

Driving down with Taylor Swift,
Gosh, feeling really adrift.
I feel the upside-down sky.
No questions but what, how, where, when, why.

Skating down that crumbly road,
Not knowing in what mode.
The way just isn't clear,
Filled with unknowns, nowhere to steer.

Of course, going on is the way,
But I also say, "What the hey!"
I don't think life is cheap.
It's powerful, strong, and deep.

Something we need to keep,
So get with the outspoken show,
Get with all that you know,
And follow the signs which say "Go!"

DUST TO HEART

My caring is becoming increasingly sparing,
Going out the door, the loss of caring.
Trouble comes in with a wind so cold,
Shivers down the back, trembling bold.

Who knows what, why, when, where?
Who knows freedom, love, and share?
Falling downstairs so fast,
Broken, disheveled to the last.

When it flies away so much,
The hurt goes right into every touch.
There is no holding,
Just folding, folding, folding.

Maybe there's nothing left to understand,
Nothing bright, nothing grand.
There's that ditch on the side of the road.
Is that my place as the story's told?

BREATH

Rays of sunshine
Appear on the horizon.
How delicate are they?
Can we hold on to them?
We must—to give hope,
To give breath
To the life of our
Precious one.
To give chances of love
For all of us.

Poem to My Father

Is the rain washing away the tears or
Is it creating more tears?
Are we breaking our hearts or
Are we having our hearts broken?
Down the gullies,
Through the forest,
Washing, washing, taking away our sorrows?
Do we know what we see, hear, taste, smell, or touch?
Can we part of this beautiful world,
Or must we carry this heaviness throughout our lives?
Are we facing reality in front of our faces or
Are we running from what will catch us in the end?
Life is as precious as every single drop of rain,
Every grain of sand,
Every star in the sky,
Every leaf on the tree,
And every soul on this planet.

HOPE

If there ever was an ounce of hope,
Please come now and make yourself known.
We really need you
To grow from an ounce to a pound to a ton
To many tons.
Somewhere in the sky,
There is a tiny brightness, a minute shine
That needs to glow and glow,
Enveloping, broadening,
Coming out of the dark, stormy clouds of despair.
Somewhere, please show yourself, know yourself, be yourself,
And give us that ledge to hold on to.

I have places to go, promises to keep,
And miles to go before I sleep.

WHITE DOVE

Could that white dove of love please appear at the window?
Don't fly away.
Stay, not just for a while,
But really stay—
Stay with this day and keep staying.
Point your wings in our direction,
Our life which is his life.
We need you,
We call upon you.
Come forth and show yourself,
Your love, your strength,
Your lasting heart.

ROLL OF THE DICE

The dice are rolled.
Double sixes came up.
Two losses,
Two ways.
He lost.
We lost.
But also, the world lost.
Snake eyes,
The worst hand.
Deadly hand—
No chance.
No way
Could we say
That today
There was another way.
Life has been taken.
Our lives have been shaken.
Nothing will be the same.
Who's to blame?
The game was over before it began.
Our love cries out with pain!
Can't you give us more to keep our hearts tame?

How I Feel

The sun may be shining so beautifully,
But you can't see it.
The air may be crisp and clean,
But you can't feel it.
The grass may be soft and green,
But you can't smell it.
The birds may be singing their cheery songs,
But you can't hear them.
Sugary blossoms may float in the air,
But you can't taste them.
When the heart is heavy and
The pain goes past your soul,
Your world doesn't travel
Past your own being.

DEMON OF DEATH

How can you dare to stand above us?
We will not allow it.
We will not make it happen.
You will come down.
We'll see to it that you come down.
We will bring you down.
We will do everything in our power
To stop you, hold you down, disengage you,
Remove your power, and
End your presence once and for all.
We will utilize every resource available,
Every fiber in our bodies,
Every cell of our being,
And every notion in our brains
To obliterate you and
All evil that surrounds you.
Our determination to win is at the highest level.
We will succeed.

NEXT

How can I touch down
When I am flying so high
Away from all the treacherous road of pain?
It's all there waiting for me
To travel along its winding, bumpy,
Soul-jarring, stabbing point-by-point way.
It's no way today.
What you say won't delay.
What we pray won't take away
The blinding light,
The flash of darkness,
The gray cloud descending on our human spirit.
It rests on our shoulders,
Pressing down, pushing us to the ground
So that we can't get back up.
How can we get up and stand up?
Will it take a miracle?
Yes, but no.
It will take raw human courage,
The reaching into our soul,
To bring forth the morsel of dignity that lies within all of
us,
That spark of brightness that will carry us through this
time
Of human disbelief.

From Paradise to Hell in a Few Hours

So what is it like to go from paradise to
Hell in a few hours?
It's from the highest high
To the lowest low.
It's from the widest smile to
The deepest furrow of sadness in your face.
It's from the highest point on earth
To the lowest point in the ocean.
It's from the first trillionth of a second
When the Big Bang set in motion
The atoms of life,
To the burning out of our sun billions of years from now.
Of course, you can't really put it into words.
You have to do it,
See it go through the pores of your skin,
The actual membranes of your body,
The cells of your being into your soul.

CASCADE

When I turned on the light this morning,
I thought blood was pouring out,
Cascading over the room.
But within moments, the blood became light.
The light was the light,
The feeling, the thought inside
Was the blood manifesting as the light.
It was pure pain expressed in that form.
I want to get through that pain, that blood,
But I know it will take time.
Even if the blood appears again,
I want the strength to go through it,
Defeat it, and go on to do what must be done.
Many painful steps,
Exhausting, nauseating, stabbing to the bone,
Heartrending, weakening.
But necessary steps—
They must be accomplished,
Completed, dealt with,
One by one
Over these hurdles in the marathon of directives.
The weight of my legs is so heavy,
Yet I must keep walking.
My legs are in pain from the top of my feet
To the bottom—pain, pain, pain.
I must keep going, ignore the pain.
There is so much to be done.

MORE

It was a springtime of sadness,
Where gladness took a backseat.
When the bright lilies and blooms sprang forth to what?
We could not hold them in our hands,
We did not feel them warming our hearts.
The sweet scent of bursting blossoms
Could not touch our noses.
We were aware of the vibrant beauty that we were a part of.
It did not penetrate the layer of pain and sadness
That gripped our souls these days.
Perhaps over time
A tiny shoot,
A baby seedling,
A microscopic element of life
Will venture forth
Into our existence and
Show light so we can see.

My Heart Burns

Why have you dared to take over my heart, our hearts?
I hate you with a passion
That is so deep
That its fire burns at infinite degrees.
A passion so deep that the Big Bang
Is like a popgun blast.
A passion so deep that time can't fathom it on any scale
Known to mankind at this moment.

THE MARCH OF LIGHT

I observe this march of light—
What is its core,
Its being,
Its essence,
Its innermost soul,
Its untold story of all time?
Why are you torturing me?
What have I done to disturb
Your endless march,
Your path,
Your ongoing cycle?
Is it madness
Or cold, calculating murder?
A killing done with no forethought
Nor any afterthought.
A dying sound that is unheard by anyone—
Even within close range.
A squeezing of breath that
Has no chance to get out or get in.
Can someone be so heartless,
So cold, so mean, so inhuman?
Why, yes, said the unsmiling man.
Yes, and yes again.
In fact, countless times.
Now, then, and again,
Once, twice, a million billion times over and over.
It will go on
Unless something is done.
The answer appears,
But the hazy fog of deception, falsehoods, travesty, and
innuendo
Cover my eyes.
But not my brain!

PIECES OF NUMB

No one can know the depth
Of pain, hurt, sorrow, anguish, mortification,
Emptiness, sadness rendering internally,
Heartbreak, numbness, and anger
That we feel at these given moments—
These charged seconds of minutes turned hours,
Turned day-week-month-year,
When time takes over—
But does it really?
It only covers with a thin veneer,
Which can be broken at the drop of a hat—
Shattered into billions of pieces,
Scattered to the four winds,
Impossible to pick up,
Or be seen,
Yet to be felt absolutely.

MELTING REALITY

Memory melts reality,
Transfers into consciousness,
Without subconscious knowledge,
But always feeling, feeling, feeling.
How can the bells ring,
Yet I can't hear them?
How can the birds sing when
I can't follow their tunes?
How do the bees buzz
When I miss their purpose?
When the sky shines blue and
The leaves scream their green,
I am still hollow inside,
Afraid to reveal the deafening echo,
Which resounds,
Bouncing off the walls,
And into the recesses of my brain.
I am waiting for the restoration
Of my humanity.
Waiting, waiting.
The silence is deafening, probing,
Penetrating my consciousness.
Down that alley of never-ending, nerve-wracking madness,
Sprinkled with a dose of self-pity,
And tortured manipulation,
As the corkscrew of searing pain
Is convoluted with an enveloping sky of rage,
We pause.
But only for a microsecond
To see if that one step can lead to a different
End unto itself.

CRY

A kaleidoscope of torture
Cascading in the body and brain,
Rendering the tips of all appendages
With crystalline daggers.
Do we not bleed,
Do we not cry,
Do we not endure,
This horrendous suffering?
Yes, but we proclaim
Somewhere, somehow, sometime, and
In some manner
A voice,
A cry in the woods.
But is anyone listening?

A LIFETIME

What you do in a second
Can last a lifetime.
What you do in a lifetime
Can last a second.
Time immemorial can be cruel
To the human soul.
So we preserve it for living,
Life, the breath of air we take
To go on in our daily routine.
We take advantage of our living
To continue loving, caring, giving, hoping, and being.
Existence itself must necessitate
A constant, consistent reminder
To preserve all the beauty,
The essence of triumph,
Which exudes from our pores,
And the most wonderful vision of time,
Seen throughout our brains.

ECHOES OF SILENCE

The languishing echoes of silence
Interpenetrate the throes of our passion—
Reverberating,
Acting independently without true meaning,
Yet hurtful, nevertheless.
What a conflict between the righteous levels of being
And the downward spiral of wall closing oppression!
The fight is on.
The lines are drawn.
The gloves are off.
I'm throwing it down.
I pledge all my life to the fight, the battle, and
Ultimately the war against all evil that exists.

What Came Through

What came through, I don't think you saw.
You didn't know what simmered beneath the skin,
Waiting to emerge like a coiled serpent
Ready to strike and what?
Take a piece, a half, a whole
Of my being?
I don't think so.
No way.
You're not going there.
I'm preparing a massive counterattack.
My hair is standing on end.
My skin is crawling with desire.
I'm ready to turn the tables and
Throw down with the boys, the girls, the men, the women,
The day-to-day people.
You will not be able to rip me away
From my path—
The rising horizon of life which lies before us.
Don't stand in my way!
I am moving forward with a strength that is unquenchable and
Imbued with absolute energy.

EVERY STEP

Every step she takes,
Every move she makes,
I worry.
Every breath she takes,
Every direction she stakes,
I worry.
Will she be okay today?
Who will say?
What will this picture portray?
When can we stop this infernal rattle?
Where is life with which we grapple?
How does the searing feeling of wondering
How the sky turns into earth arise within us?

EVERY NIGHT

Every night the songbird sings.
Every night the tolling bell rings.
What the future has wrought,
No one can say our soul was taught.
Every lesson has been learned.
Every twig on our branch burned.
Our inner being keeps seeing,
Knowing our eye takes aim
As we lay our bodies down to blame.
No shelter can hold and keep,
No arms can grip so deep.
The snow has risen from the top.
I know my heart cannot stop.

Fountain of Youth

Hey, I've been searching,
Searching for that Fountain of Youth.
Oh, sorry, you took a wrong turn, buddy.
You found the Fountain of Death.
It's really different from that other fountain.
As there's no turning back.
No deposit.
No return.
The desert wasteland of undaunted feelings
Where youth was not found,
Rather lost, bruised, and battered—
As a pirate ship cast adrift in that murky sea,
Facing that precision machine aimed
At the soul of our breath.
Do you want to escape from hell?
Well, we all do.
But some just don't know how.
There's not a simple answer.
It won't just appear in the moonlight,
Jump out of the fire bright,
Or climb into your bed at night.
It can come to you in a dream,
A vision grounded in the down-to-earth
Reality of our existence—
The bare essence of motion and love in all its glory.

LITTLE SPARROW IN THE RAIN

What does that little sparrow think?
About what to eat and what to drink?
Perhaps meeting a friend to fly and fly
Or resting and nesting by and by.

Can little brains have big thoughts
About lessons learned and movements taught?
Or just asking why, why, and why,
Can't we just try, try, and try?

Are you there for all of us,
Or do we have doubt where we should trust?
Do we not live to preserve all the good
And give to nature and humanity all that we should?

SLEEP

Oh sleep, oh sleep,
We all need you—light or deep.
Come easy, come hard,
Depending upon the turn of the card.

Why are you sometimes so fitful
And otherwise so calm and restful?
We breathe in, we breathe out.
Sometimes we even give a shout.

Can you come to us without that pill?
Can you stay longer and sweeter still?
We want to hold onto your being
Even with all the dreams we are seeing.

The Towers of Babel are quiet now.
We're done with the where, when, and how.
So close your beautiful eyes,
And tomorrow with peace you'll be worldly wise.

LEAVES

Leaves, oh leaves, do you have a story,
About life and love with all its glory?
Are you small and soft as a whisper
Or brittle, crackling crisper?

Your colors give away your seasons
About faith and nature with reasons.
Have you traveled far or fallen near?
Have you touched someone's heart so dear?

Are you in a pile for jumping
Or just being hauled away for dumping?
Will you come back fragile and new
As the baby seedling so true?

Don't fly away and leave me.
Please stay around and kiss the tree.
Where you go,
I will not know,
But I will miss you—oh no!

TIME

We can't live with it.
We can't live without it.
On it goes and goes and goes,
Forward or back, fast or slow—everyone knows.

We dive into that zone.
We don't stop on the phone.
It's ours, but not our own.
We question what has been shown.

BC, AD, the here and now—
Past, present, future—wow!
Where did it all go?
So what do we really know?   .

Feeling or believing,
Achieving or conceiving,
We must go on riding that wave,
For it's our earth and our love we will save.

Hugs

Why is it that hugs are so great?
Why are they worth their weight
In gold?
Well, you know, they never grow old.

Is it the tender warmth that hugs provide,
Or the meaning, the feeling inside?
Yes, all of the above and more,
They open the human door.

Relatives, friends, comrades all,
Open your arms, break down that wall.
Reach out and hold your fellow being.
Open your eyes beyond what you are seeing.

A simple, yet beautiful act,
A journey of one's soul, a basic fact.
When you connect and surround,
You join a better world so profound.

SCRABBLE

If you dabble
In Scrabble,
You need to know your words,
And be down-to-earth, not with the birds.

Oh my, did you get that triple score?
Do you know more and more and more?
Did you use letters—all the seven?
Did it feel like a slice of heaven?

Maybe we don't need that dictionary
As you have such a huge vocabulary.
We can feel our brains heating
With all the great words we are meeting.

Come one, come all—
Scrabble is such a ball.
We can play hours on end.
It's some of the best time we can spend.

SERENA WITH GRACE

Serena—are you a dreama?
No, you are the one with grace and style,
One who always goes the extra mile,
One who always has that infectious smile.

Your strength cannot be denied.
You stand strong—showing that pride.
Your style is there with each stride.
Your skill is true and tried.

With that quiet, focused look,
You are rewriting the tennis history book.
You keep looking up, not down.
We see the joy in what you have found.

Keep going ahead and ahead,
Keep filling those pages we have read.
You must be that one on top,
The one no one can stop.

LIFE ON THE RUN

What if you are on the run,
Traveling at night away from the sun?
Your identity must change,
Your daily pattern must rearrange.

Your life is not the same,
So adapt to this new game.
Change your lifestyle now.
Transform your appearance somehow.

What about your family, your friends,
The constant beginnings without ends?
You can't communicate very much,
And always beware of any touch.

Do what you must today and tomorrow.
Contain and control any of your sorrow.
Survival is an absolute must.
Now you are the only one you can trust.

ACCIDENT

That jarring moment, that instant,
When all is asunder and strangely distant.
The splintering, the shattering, the flash,
Thundering, stinging, echo of the crash.

A life-changing piece of time,
Blinding, binding,
No reason or rhyme,
Winding, grinding.

Is the blood yours or mine?
Are you okay, are you just fine?
Can you get out?
Can you give a shout?

Gather your thoughts, focus your mind.
Reach inside, use all you can find.
Save yourself, save the other.
Survive and look out for one another.

EXPECTATION

What is it when you expect
And then you don't get
What you wanted
As though you're being taunted?

That one thing, that one desire,
Maybe some bling or what's inside you like fire.
Were you given a choice,
Or being ignored, silencing your voice?

In the pit of your stomach, you are feeling,
A wish that is so appealing.
Something with which you are dealing
As what you want has no ceiling.

No denying what's rightfully your own,
So stand up, let your wishes be known.
Time to get what you expect,
Time to be treated with respect.

CONVERGENCE

A particular time,
Without rhythm or rhyme,
Events and people meet,
Prediction takes a seat.

A profundity,
An entity,
Of light and dark,
Of clear sight—standing stark.

History in the making,
Steps we are taking,
To seize and hold,
To never let go, to be so bold.

As pieces come together,
Sights and sounds merge without a tether.
Connections are plain to see.
Our hearts beat as one
To be free and to be done.

THE STUDY

Approaching that special room,
The contents one can only assume.
Does it hold treasures of the past?
Does it contain memories that will always last?

I know about the Nobel prizes
And the stories of Rescue heroes on the rise.
The thesis, the texts, the diaries galore,
The videos, the paintings, the drawings, and more.

This sanctum embedded with history,
Uncovering truths, no longer a mystery.
A life which touched so many lives,
Knowledge and understanding so worldly-wise.

Dare I go further into this world,
Dare I reach and find such blossoms unfurled.
Yes, and yes again I will go ahead,
So my heart will no longer lightly tread.

AND IT RAINED UPON THE LAND

When love is at stake,
We will do whatever it takes
To move mountains, lakes.
Like I said, whatever it takes.

You must ground your belief
To find what gives relief
To that loved one,
Making sure that it is done.

We must go on with life,
Free from pain and strife.
Get with the power to be,
What and whom will set us free.

Go forth, young people, and see
The beauty of the flower, the tree.
We all sacrifice and give our soul
To reach that yet attainable goal.

HELP YOURSELF

How can you help others
If you can't even help yourself?
How can you be your own center
When you don't see the circle around you?
Thinking of only me, myself, and I
Ends up as that inauspicious little fly.
When does caring begin?
When should it end?
The one and only would not exist
If it weren't for the two and only.
History is not made by that one over there,
But rather by all bound in common
In the clenched expression of emotion and humanity.

THE SOUNDS

Move over, Simon and Garfunkel,
I do hear the sounds of silence.
The violin legs of those chirpers,
The ruby ovals of those frog throats.
Hey, little fellows, I really do need some sleep,
To drift and not too deep.
I'd like a hand to hold,
A shoulder maybe, soft or bold.
A gesture of warmth and care,
Lounging in the atmosphere of fair.
Love conquers all,
I've been told.
So let's move on that thought—
Let's turn it into gold.
We want that pure show—
That inner depth to glow.
Might really does not make right.
It's our passion that's in our mind's sight.
Bring out the clowns,
Throw down the frowns.
No need to languish in the fear,
Let's pull together all that's dear.
Our present status must rise above,
Reveal ourselves without the glove.
Time calls for all to move.
It's okay if you don't fit the groove.
We can each have our turn,
Give and take, love and learn.
Beauty is in the eye of all.
Our soul is here and now, hear the call.

FOR LOVE

The question today is,
What will you do for love?
Will you sit back and let it just happen?
Will you go out and make that effort,
That effect,
That reason,
That show of true belief?
I will stake everything I know, believe, think, feel,
Understand, carry, perceive, grasp, and embrace,
For love.
The ultimate on this earth—
This paradise for humanity,
Which against all odds must be based on love.
As the song goes, "Love don't come easy."
No, it certainly doesn't come easy!
But we stake our lives on it.
What are you willing to do for love?
We must endure,
We must sacrifice,
Give our spirit to the ultimate line drawn on the ground.
We will give all so that the generations
Will live, breathe, and love.

CPSIA information can be obtained at www.ICGtesting.com
Printed in the USA
BVOW071613080812

297357BV00002B/87/P